MIDLIFE
A TRUE JOURNEY

TERRY GRIFFITHS

BESTLIFEISMIDLIFE

kindle direct publishing

ISBN: 9798854863780

MIDLIFE A True Journey

Copyright © 2023 Terry Griffiths (bestlifeismidlife)

All rights reserved. This book or parts thereof may not be reproduced in any form, stored in any retrieval system, or transmitted in any form by any means—electronic, mechanical, photocopy, recording, or otherwise—without prior written permission of the publisher.

ISBN: 9798854863780

kdp.amazon.com

bestlifeismidlife.com

MIDLIFE A True Journey

Table Of Contents

Chapter 1: Exploring Your Midlife Wakeup Call: Understanding the Journey of Self-Discovery   **11**

The Midlife Crisis Phenomenon: Debunking Myths and Embracing Realities   11

The Role of Self-Reflection: Assessing Your Current Situation at home and at work, don't feel guilty for past mistakes.   14

Navigating the Emotional Rollercoaster: Coping with Midlife Crisis and what not to do.   16

Seeking Support: Building a Network of Allies and Mentors, partner support and family   19

It's OK to be you, introverted but proud of it. Should not worry what others think of you, you are unique.   21

Chapter 2: Career Change: Finding Fulfilment and Purpose in the Second Half of Life   **24**

Recognising the Signs: Identifying the Need for a Career Change   24

Assessing Your Skills and Interests: Uncovering Hidden Passions — 26

Exploring New Career Paths: Researching Opportunities, Industries or creating your own business. — 29

Overcoming Obstacles: Dealing with Fear, Doubt, and Financial Concerns — 32

Chapter 3: Financial Instability: Overcoming Challenges and Achieving Stability — **35**

Evaluating Your Financial Situation: Understanding the Impact of Midlife Crisis — 35

Overcoming the cost of living crisis, how to make another income stream and save money — 37

Developing a Financial Plan: Budgeting, Saving, and Investing for the Future — 39

Exploring Entrepreneurship: Starting a Business or Side hustle. — 42

Seeking Professional Help: Financial Advisors and Resources for Midlife Crisis — 45

Chapter 4: Health and Wellness: Prioritising Self-Care and Wellbeing — **47**

Assessing Your Physical Health: Understanding the Impact of Midlife Crisis	47
Ageing symptoms beyond your control	49
Embracing Healthy Habits: Nutrition, Exercise, and Self-Care Practices to keep your internal fat low and be healthier to avoid aging illnesses like heart conditions and diabetes.	52
Addressing Mental Health: Managing Stress, Anxiety, and Depression with and without your doctor	55
Is taking pills the only option for mental illness or can self help methods work	58
Exploring Alternative Therapies: Yoga, Meditation, and Mindfulness	61
Chapter 5: Acquiring New Skills: Upskilling and Adapting to the Changing Job Market	**64**
Identifying In-Demand Skills: Researching Job Market Trends	64
Pursuing Continuing Education: Online digital Courses, and Certification Programs	66

Leveraging Transferable Skills: Applying Existing
Knowledge to New Opportunities and learn new
digital skills.   69

How easy is it to start a business in digital marketing,
affiliate marketing is a great place to start and what it
is.   71

Networking and Mentorship: Building Connections in
Your Desired Field   73

**Chapter 6: Retirement Concerns: Planning for
Financial Security and a Meaningful Future**   **76**

Rethinking Retirement: Redefining the Concept in
the Midlife Crisis Era   76

Developing a Retirement Plan: Investing, Saving,
and Budgeting for the Future   78

What is the average government pension and will it
be enough to live on when you retire?   81

Exploring Retirement Options: Part-Time Work,
Volunteering, and creating a passive online income   83

Creating a Fulfilling Retirement: Balancing Leisure,
Hobbies, and Personal Growth   86

Chapter 7: Midlife Crisis in Different Professions: Challenges and Solutions for Public Sector Workers, Retail Employees, and Those who deal with the public   **89**

Midlife Crisis in the Public Sector: Navigating Bureaucracy and Seeking New Opportunities   89

Transitioning from Retail to a New Career: Transferable Skills and Job Market Analysis   92

Surviving Midlife Crisis in a job outside the 9-5 Industry: Reinventing Yourself in a Changing Market   94

From Retail Manager to Successful Entrepreneur: My Journey Through Midlife Crisis   96

No technical skill can be learnt and is essential as the world is changing, how Ai is transforming the world it is today and jobs are going in certain industries.   99

Chapter 8: Embracing the Journey: Finding Confidence, Purpose, and Happiness in Midlife Crisis   **101**

Building Self-Confidence: Overcoming Doubts and Embracing Change   101

Self belief through Midlife   103

Self-doubt through Midlife   105

Embracing Failure at Midlife: Learning and Growing from Setbacks — 107

Avoid Procrastination — 109

Discovering Your Purpose: Aligning Values, Passions, and Career Choices — 111

Cultivating Happiness: Finding Joy and Contentment in the Midlife Journey — 113

Creating a Meaningful Life: Balancing Career, Relationships, and Personal Growth — 114

Chapter 9: Midlife Questions? — **117**

Top 30 Questions to reflect back on your life so far. — 117

What now, What's on your bucket list? — 120

Chapter 1: Exploring Your Midlife Wakeup Call: Understanding the Journey of Self-Discovery

The Midlife Crisis Phenomenon: Debunking Myths and Embracing Realities

Introduction:

As we enter our 40s and beyond, many of us question our choices, goals, and overall satisfaction with life. This stage is commonly known as the midlife crisis, a term that often conjures negative connotations and misconceptions. However, we will debunk these myths and shed light on the realities of the midlife crisis phenomenon. We will explore how it relates to career change, financial freedom, retirement concerns, and health, focusing on the nuances of the midlife crisis, self-discovery, economic instability, and health and wellness.

Debunking the Myths: Contrary to popular belief, the midlife crisis is not a universal experience characterised by impulsive behaviour and emotional turmoil. It is a complex and deeply personal journey that varies from person to person. While some may face internal conflicts and reevaluate their choices, others embrace this stage as an opportunity for self-discovery and growth. Understanding that the midlife crisis is not an adverse event but a natural part of the human experience is crucial.

Navigating Career Change:

For many individuals, the midlife crisis prompts a revaluation of their career paths. The desire for a more fulfilling and meaningful job becomes paramount. We will provide practical advice and strategies for those considering a career change in their 40s and beyond. We will explore the challenges and rewards of transitioning into new industries. Moreover, we will emphasise the importance of acquiring new skills and adapting to the demands of a rapidly changing job market.

Financial Freedom and Retirement Concerns: Midlife crisis and financial instability often go hand in hand. This subchapter will address the common concerns surrounding retirement planning, including financial security and the fear of running out of money. We will guide you on managing financial resources effectively, investing wisely, and creating a solid retirement plan. By debunking the myth that it is too late to achieve financial freedom in midlife, we will inspire readers to take control of their financial future.

Midlife Crisis and Health and Wellness: The midlife crisis can also significantly affect one's physical and mental well-being. We will explore the link between midlife crisis and health, emphasising the importance of self-care, stress management, and maintaining a healthy lifestyle. We will delve into various wellness practices, including yoga, meditation, and other forms of exercise that can help individuals navigate this challenging phase with resilience and vitality.

Conclusion: We have debunked the myths surrounding the midlife crisis phenomenon and highlighted the realities faced by men and women over 40. By providing insights into career change, financial freedom, retirement concerns, and health and wellness, we aim to empower our readers with the knowledge and tools necessary to embrace this transformative stage of life. Let us navigate the midlife journey together and emerge stronger, wiser, and more fulfilled.

The Role of Self-Reflection: Assessing Your Current Situation at home and at work, don't feel guilty for past mistakes.

In the journey of life, there comes a time when we reach a crossroads, a moment of self-reflection that forces us to assess our current situation. For men and women in their 40s and beyond, this period of self-discovery is commonly known as the midlife crisis. However, it is essential to understand that this phase is not just about crisis but also an opportunity for growth, career change, and financial freedom.

At this stage, many individuals find themselves questioning their choices and decisions. They may feel stuck in careers that no longer bring them fulfilment, plagued by financial concerns, or struggling with health and wellness issues. The key to navigating this midlife journey lies in self-reflection, where you take the time to evaluate your current situation and make necessary changes.

Assessing your current situation at home and work is vital as it allows you to identify areas needing improvement. Step back and ask yourself, "Am I content with my career? Do I have a healthy work-life balance? Are my financial goals being met? Is my health being prioritized?" By answering these questions, you can gain valuable insights into what needs to change and where to focus your energy.

It is crucial not to feel guilty for past mistakes during this process. The midlife crisis is not about dwelling on the past but learning from it. Embrace the lessons you have learned and use them as stepping stones towards a brighter future. Remember, there is always time to change and pursue a career that brings you joy and financial stability.

This could be the perfect time to explore new skills and opportunities. Consider leveraging your experience and knowledge to embark on a new path. You may have always dreamt of starting your own business, becoming a yoga instructor, or pursuing a career in a different field. The possibilities are endless.

In conclusion, self-reflection is crucial when navigating the midlife journey. Assessing your current situation at home and work allows you to make informed decisions and take necessary steps towards a fulfilling and prosperous future. Please don't feel guilty for past mistakes; instead, embrace them as valuable lessons that have shaped you. Remember, this is your opportunity for self-discovery, career change, financial freedom, and enhanced health and wellness. Embrace the journey and create the life you desire.

Navigating the Emotional Rollercoaster: Coping with Midlife Crisis and what not to do.

Introduction:

Entering the midlife phase can be a tumultuous journey filled with emotional ups and downs, commonly known as the midlife crisis. In this subchapter, we will explore the various challenges that individuals in their 40s and beyond face during this period and provide valuable insights on how to cope with these challenges. We will also discuss what not to do to ensure a smoother transition into this new phase of life.

Understanding the Midlife Crisis:

The midlife crisis is a natural response to the realisation. That time is passing by, and individuals may experience a sense of dissatisfaction with their current life circumstances. It often manifests as restlessness, anxiety, and the need for change.

Coping Strategies:

1. Self-reflection: Take the time to reflect on your life, values, and goals. This introspection will help you gain a better understanding of what you truly desire and what changes you need to make to achieve fulfilment.

2. Seek support: Surround yourself with a supportive network of friends, family, or even a therapist who can provide guidance and a listening ear during this challenging period.

3. Embrace change: Instead of resisting change, embrace it as an opportunity for growth and self-discovery. Consider exploring new career paths, hobbies, or even travel experiences that can reignite your passion and zest for life.

What not to do:

1. Impulsive decision-making: Avoid making impulsive decisions that may have long-lasting consequences. Instead, take the time to carefully evaluate your options and seek advice from trusted professionals before making any major life changes.

2. Neglecting financial planning: Midlife crisis can often coincide with concerns about financial stability and retirement. It is crucial to prioritise financial planning during this phase to ensure a secure future.

3. Ignoring health and wellness: Midlife crisis can take a toll on your physical and mental well-being. Don't neglect your health; instead, prioritise self-care activities such as regular exercise, healthy eating, and stress management techniques like yoga or meditation.

Conclusion: Navigating the emotional rollercoaster of a midlife crisis can be challenging. Still, with the right coping strategies and a proactive approach, it can also be a period of self-discovery and personal growth. By avoiding impulsive decisions, prioritising financial planning, and taking care of your health, you can successfully navigate this transformative phase and emerge more robust and fulfilled on the other side. Remember, the midlife crisis can be an opportunity for positive change and a chance to create your desired life.

Seeking Support: Building a Network of Allies and Mentors, partner support and family

In navigating the midlife journey, one of the most crucial aspects is seeking support from a strong network of allies and mentors. We explore the importance of building such a network and the specific challenges and opportunities faced by men and women over 40 in the realms of career change, financial freedom, retirement concerns, and more.

For those experiencing a midlife crisis, the need for support becomes even more pressing. This chapter delves into the unique struggles faced during this transformative period. It provides insights on how to find solace and self-discovery amidst the chaos. It emphasizes the significance of seeking guidance from mentors who have experienced similar challenges and emerged stronger on the other side.

Recognising that a midlife crisis often brings financial instability, we will address career change and financial freedom concerns. Additionally, it highlights the importance of acquiring new skills to stay competitive in today's rapidly changing job market.

Furthermore, this chapter acknowledges the growing emphasis on health and wellness during the midlife crisis. It explores the link between mental well-being and career satisfaction, providing strategies for maintaining balance and finding fulfilment. Whether it's yoga, meditation, or other self-care practices, this subchapter offers valuable insights on incorporating health and wellness into the midlife journey.

Partner support and family play a vital role in navigating the midlife journey. This section delves into the dynamics of these relationships and offers guidance on building a solid support system. It addresses the concerns and challenges faced by those going through a midlife crisis, providing tips on effective communication, understanding, and empathy.

In conclusion, seeking support is crucial when facing a midlife crisis or embarking on a journey of self-discovery and career change. This subchapter provides valuable insights and practical advice for men and women over 40, regardless of their specific niche or profession. Individuals can successfully navigate the midlife journey and emerge more robust and fulfilled by building a network of allies and mentors, finding partner support, and nurturing family relationships.

It's OK to be you, introverted but proud of it. Should not worry what others think of you, you are unique.

Introversion is often misunderstood and undervalued in our society, which tends to favour extroverted qualities. Many people mistakenly believe that being introverted is a flaw or something to be ashamed of. However, in the subchapter titled "It's OK to be you, introverted but proud of it," we aim to debunk these misconceptions and empower individuals to embrace their unique introverted nature.

For men and women over 40 who are experiencing a midlife crisis or contemplating a career change, it is crucial to understand that introversion is not a hindrance but a strength—being introverted means having a rich inner world, being reflective, and having the ability to think deeply and critically. These qualities can be invaluable when navigating through the complexities of a midlife crisis.

In a society that often values constant socialising and networking, introverted individuals might feel pressured to conform and worry about what others think of them. However, it is essential to remember that you are unique and that your introverted nature makes you unique. Embrace your introversion proudly, without concern for the opinions of others.

Moreover, being introverted does not mean lacking social skills or being incapable of forming meaningful connections. Many introverts excel in one-on-one interactions and possess excellent listening skills, making them great partners, friends, and colleagues. By embracing your introverted nature, you can leverage these strengths and build authentic relationships that align with your values and interests.

Furthermore, introversion can also be advantageous regarding financial freedom and retirement concerns. While extroverts may be more inclined to seek external validation through material possessions, introverts tend to be more introspective and focus on their long-term financial goals. By being true to yourself and not succumbing to societal pressures, you can make financial decisions that align with your values and provide you with the security and peace of mind you desire.

Embracing your introversion can bring about positive changes. Introverts often excel in roles that require deep focus, critical thinking, and attention to detail. By honing your unique introverted qualities, you can discover new skills and excel in your chosen field, ultimately leading to personal and professional growth.

In conclusion, it is crucial to embrace your introverted nature proudly and not worry about what others think of you. You are unique, and your introversion is a strength that can lead to self-discovery, financial stability, and overall well-being. By acknowledging and valuing your introversion, you can confidently navigate your midlife crisis and create a fulfilling and purposeful life.

Chapter 2: Career Change: Finding Fulfilment and Purpose in the Second Half of Life

Recognising the Signs: Identifying the Need for a Career Change

Are you feeling stuck in your current job, longing for a change but unsure if it's the right move for you? You're not alone if you're over 40 and experiencing these thoughts. Many men and women in their middle age find themselves at a crossroads, questioning their career choices and seeking a path towards self-discovery, financial freedom, and overall fulfilment.

We will explore the signs that indicate it may be time for a career change. Whether you are a public sector worker, retail employee, tourism professional, or health practitioner, these signs can universally apply to anyone seeking a new direction.

One of the most common signals of the need for a career change is a sense of stagnation or boredom in your current role. You may find yourself going through the motions without feeling challenged or motivated. This lack of enthusiasm can lead to decreased productivity and overall job satisfaction.

Financial concerns are another significant factor that can trigger the need for a career change. As you approach middle age, thoughts of retirement become more prominent. If you're worried about your financial stability in the future, consider a change that can provide you with the means to secure your retirement and achieve long-term financial freedom.

Your health and well-being can also play a significant role in recognising the need for a career change. Midlife is a critical time to prioritize your physical and mental health. Suppose your current job is causing excessive stress, burnout, or negatively impacting your overall well-being. In that case, it's essential to acknowledge these signs and explore alternative paths that prioritise your health and wellness.

Furthermore, acquiring new skills and interests can catalyse a career change. Your perspectives and passions may evolve as you age, and you may discover new fields or industries that excite you. Embracing these new interests and seeking opportunities to develop new skills can clearly indicate that it's time to pursue a different career path.

Recognising the signs that point towards a necessary career change is crucial no matter what niche you identify with. The midlife crisis can be a transformative period, offering a chance for self-discovery, financial stability, and improved health and well-being. By paying attention to the signs and taking action, you can navigate the midlife journey and embark on a fulfilling and rewarding career journey.

Assessing Your Skills and Interests: Uncovering Hidden Passions

Introduction: As we navigate through midlife, many find ourselves at a crossroads, contemplating career change, seeking financial freedom, or worrying about retirement concerns. Whatever your current career, we will help you uncover your hidden passions and guide you towards a fulfilling path in life. Through self-assessment, exploration, and acquiring new skills, we can embrace midlife as an opportunity for self-discovery and personal growth.

Assessing Your Skills:

One of the first steps in uncovering your hidden passions is to assess your current skills and interests. Take some time to reflect on your past experiences, both personal and professional. What tasks or activities have you enjoyed the most? What skills have you developed over the years? Identifying your strengths and weaknesses can help you narrow down potential career paths and areas of interest.

Uncovering Your Interests: It's essential to explore new interests and hobbies. Consider taking up new activities that pique your curiosity, such as yoga, painting, or cooking. These activities can open new doors and provide valuable insights into what truly brings you joy. Additionally, connecting with like-minded individuals through local clubs or online communities can lead to new opportunities and collaborations.

Embracing Self-Discovery: Midlife crisis often catalyses self-discovery. Use this transformative period to delve deeper into your values, beliefs, and aspirations. Reflect on what truly matters to you and what you want to achieve in the next chapter of your life. This introspection will help you align your passions with your long-term goals, leading to a more purposeful and fulfilling career.

Acquiring New Skills: As you uncover your hidden passions, you must acquire new skills that align with your interests. Embrace continuous learning by enrolling in courses, attending workshops, or seeking mentorship in your chosen field. Developing new skills enhances your expertise, boosts your confidence, and opens doors to new career opportunities.

Health and Wellness in Midlife Crisis: Midlife crisis often brings health and wellness concerns to the forefront. Taking care of your physical and mental well-being becomes crucial during this transformative period. Incorporate yoga, meditation, or regular exercise into your routine to reduce stress and increase self-awareness. Prioritising your health will empower you to navigate the challenges of midlife with resilience and vitality.

Conclusion: Uncovering your hidden passions and pursuing a fulfilling career may seem daunting during a midlife crisis. However, by assessing your skills, exploring new interests, embracing self-discovery, and acquiring new skills, you can navigate this journey with confidence and purpose. Remember, midlife is a unique opportunity for personal growth, financial freedom, and well-being. Embrace the journey, and let your hidden passions guide you towards a brighter and more fulfilling future.

Exploring New Career Paths: Researching Opportunities, Industries or creating your own business.

In our fast-paced world, it's not uncommon for individuals to find themselves at a crossroads in their careers during their 40s and beyond. Whether you're feeling unfulfilled, seeking financial freedom, or simply looking for a change, exploring new career paths can be exciting and rewarding. This subchapter will guide you through researching opportunities and industries or even creating your own business, providing valuable insights and actionable steps tailored to the unique needs and concerns of men and women in midlife.

Researching opportunities is an essential first step when considering a career change. Identifying industries that align with your interests, skills, and values is critical. This subchapter will provide tips on conducting thorough research, such as utilizing online resources, attending industry events, and networking with professionals in your desired field. We will also explore the benefits of gaining new skills or certifications to enhance marketability and open new career possibilities.

For those interested in entrepreneurship, we will delve into creating your own business. From developing a business plan to securing funding, navigating legal requirements, and marketing your brand, this subchapter will offer a comprehensive guide to help you successfully launch and grow your venture. We will also address the unique challenges and opportunities of starting a business later in life, including financial stability and retirement planning considerations.

Additionally, we will address the specific concerns of public sector workers, retail and tourism professionals, and those in the health and wellness industry. We will provide insights into leveraging your existing experience and skills in these fields to transition into new career paths or explore entrepreneurial ventures. Whether you're considering a career in yoga instruction, opening a boutique wellness centre, or venturing into a completely different industry, this subchapter will offer practical advice and inspiration.

Overall, "Exploring New Career Paths: Researching Opportunities, Industries or Creating Your Own Business" is a comprehensive and tailored guide to help men and women in midlife navigate the challenges and opportunities of career change. Whether experiencing a midlife crisis, seeking self-discovery, financial stability, or improved health and wellness, this subchapter will equip you with the knowledge and tools to make informed decisions and embark on a fulfilling and successful career journey.

Overcoming Obstacles: Dealing with Fear, Doubt, and Financial Concerns

In the journey of midlife, career change and self-discovery often go hand in hand. As we enter our 40s and beyond, it's natural to question our choices, reflect on our achievements, and contemplate our future path. However, this phase also brings along its fair share of obstacles that can hinder our progress. We will explore the everyday challenges of fear, doubt, and financial concerns that many individuals face during this transformative period.

Fear is a powerful emotion that can paralyse even the most ambitious among us. The fear of the unknown, fear of failure, or fear of starting over can often hold us back from pursuing our dreams. However, it is essential to recognise that fear is a part of the process, and you can overcome this. By acknowledging our fears, analysing their root causes, and developing strategies to confront them head-on, we can gradually diminish their influence and gain the confidence to move forward.

Doubt often accompanies fear and can be equally debilitating. Doubting our abilities, questioning our decisions, and comparing ourselves to others can undermine our self-esteem and hinder our progress. To overcome doubt, we must focus on our strengths and accomplishments, surround ourselves with supportive individuals, and practice self-compassion. By embracing a growth mindset and viewing setbacks as opportunities for growth, we can overcome doubt and forge ahead on our path to self-discovery.

Financial concerns are a common obstacle faced by individuals in midlife, especially those contemplating a career change. The prospect of leaving a stable job and venturing into unfamiliar territory can be daunting, particularly when financial responsibilities, such as mortgages and retirement savings, are at stake. However, it's crucial to remember that financial freedom and fulfilment are attainable even in a new career.

By conducting thorough research, developing a financial plan, seeking guidance from professionals, and exploring opportunities for acquiring new skills, we can pave the way for a successful transition while safeguarding our financial well-being.

We will also delve into the specific concerns of public sector workers, those in retail, tourism, and health sectors, and individuals seeking new skills or exploring health and wellness options like yoga. Each niche brings its unique challenges, from navigating pension plans and transitioning from face-to-face customer service to exploring remote work options and retraining in new fields. By addressing these concerns, providing practical advice, and sharing inspiring stories of individuals who have successfully overcome similar hurdles, we aim to provide the guidance and motivation needed to navigate the midlife journey with confidence.

In conclusion, fear, doubt, and financial concerns are formidable obstacles that individuals face during midlife career change and self-discovery. However, armed with the right mindset, strategies, and resources, we can overcome these challenges and embark on a fulfilling journey of personal and professional growth. This subchapter will serve as a guide, offering insights, support, and practical tips to help men and women in their 40s and beyond navigate their unique paths towards career fulfilment, financial freedom, and a renewed sense of purpose.

Chapter 3: Financial Instability: Overcoming Challenges and Achieving Stability

Evaluating Your Financial Situation: Understanding the Impact of Midlife Crisis

In the journey of life, the midlife crisis is a stage that many individuals experience. It is a time when one starts to question their choices, desires, and the direction their life has taken. One aspect that is often impacted during this phase is an individual's financial situation. In this subchapter, we will explore the correlation between midlife crisis and financial stability, and how it affects various aspects of life including career change, retirement concerns, and health and wellness.

For men and women over 40, the midlife crisis can be a turning point in their careers. The desire for change and self-discovery often leads individuals to contemplate switching careers. However, before making any drastic decisions, it is crucial to evaluate one's financial situation. This involves assessing the current income, expenses, and savings to ensure a smooth transition without jeopardizing financial stability.

Retirement concerns are another aspect that individuals in midlife crisis often grapple with. As the realization of aging and limited working years sets in, it becomes essential to re-evaluate retirement plans. This subchapter will provide guidance on how to assess the impact of midlife crisis on retirement savings and explore strategies to ensure financial freedom during retirement.

Public sector workers, those in retail, tourism, and health-related fields, often face unique challenges during midlife crisis. This subchapter will delve into the specific concerns and provide tailored advice for these niches. It will address the potential financial implications of career changes and how to navigate them successfully.

Furthermore, a midlife crisis can affect an individual's health and well-being. Stress, anxiety, and a lack of purpose can manifest physically and mentally. This subchapter will explore the connection between midlife crisis and health, emphasising the importance of self-care and wellness practices such as yoga to alleviate stress and maintain a balanced lifestyle.

Ultimately, understanding the impact of a midlife crisis on one's financial situation is crucial for making informed decisions. This subchapter will empower individuals to evaluate their financial standing, make necessary adjustments, and holistically navigate career changes, retirement concerns, and health and wellness. Providing practical guidance and insights aims to help individuals in their journey of self-discovery, financial stability, and overall well-being during the midlife crisis.

Overcoming the cost of living crisis, how to make another income stream and save money

Introduction: Today's cost of living continues to rise, leaving many individuals in their 40s and beyond struggling to make ends meet. Whether you are facing a midlife crisis, contemplating a career change, or worried about retirement concerns, taking control of your financial future is essential. This subchapter will guide men and women over 40 through practical strategies to overcome the cost of living crisis, create additional income streams, and save money. It will also address the specific concerns of public sector workers, those in retail, tourism, and health, and individuals interested in new skills and yoga.

1. Assessing Your Financial Situation: To overcome the cost of living crisis, evaluating your current financial situation is crucial. Understand your income, expenses, and debt. Identify areas where you can cut back or eliminate unnecessary costs, such as dining out or subscription services. This assessment will lay the foundation for your journey towards financial freedom.

2. Creating Additional Income Streams: Explore various opportunities to generate additional income. For public sector workers, consider freelancing or consulting in your expertise. Retail and tourism professionals can explore online platforms to sell products or offer virtual services. Health enthusiasts can become certified fitness trainers or start a wellness blog. Embrace lifelong learning and acquire new skills that align with your passions and market demand.

3. Saving Money: Saving Money is a crucial step towards financial stability. Learn effective budgeting techniques and prioritise your expenses. Reduce utility bills, insurance premiums, and other recurring costs. Consider downsizing your living arrangements or exploring alternative housing options. You can accumulate significant savings over time by making minor adjustments and being mindful of spending habits.

4. Investing in Health and Wellness: Midlife crisis often brings a renewed focus on health and wellness. Embrace this opportunity by investing in self-care practices like yoga, meditation, and exercise. Engaging in physical activities enhances your well-being and reduces healthcare costs in the long run. Explore affordable wellness options and utilize community resources to support your journey.

Conclusion: Overcoming the cost of living crisis requires proactive steps and a commitment to financial freedom. By assessing your financial situation, creating additional income streams, saving money, and investing in health and wellness, you can navigate through the challenges of a midlife crisis and achieve stability. Remember, there is always time to take control of your financial future, no matter your career, age, or background. Start today and pave the way towards a brighter and more secure tomorrow.

Developing a Financial Plan: Budgeting, Saving, and Investing for the Future

In the ever-changing landscape of today's job market, navigating a career change in your 40s and beyond can be challenging. As you embark on this new chapter, it's essential to prioritize your financial well-being to ensure a secure future. This subchapter will guide you through developing a financial plan that encompasses budgeting, saving, and investing for the future.

Budgeting is the foundation of any successful financial plan. It involves carefully assessing your income and expenses to determine where your money is going. By creating a realistic budget, you can track your spending habits and identify areas where you can cut back. This is particularly crucial during a career change when your income may fluctuate. You can ensure financial stability throughout this transition by being mindful of your expenses.

Saving is another crucial aspect of your financial plan. As you navigate a career change, having an emergency fund is essential to handle any unexpected expenses that may arise. Aim to save at least three to six months' living expenses in a separate account. This safety net will provide you with peace of mind during this period of change.

Investing for the future is equally important, especially when considering retirement concerns. As a middle-aged individual, maximising the returns on your investments is crucial to secure your financial freedom in later years. Consider seeking guidance from a financial advisor who can help you identify the best investment opportunities that align with your goals and risk tolerance.

Public sector workers in retail, tourism, health, and other industries may face unique challenges during a career change. Understanding the financial implications of transitioning to a new field is essential. This subchapter will provide specific strategies tailored to individuals in these sectors, offering insights into leveraging existing skills, exploring new avenues, and making informed financial decisions.

Furthermore, midlife crisis is often associated with self-discovery, financial instability, and health and wellness concerns. This subchapter addresses these issues head-on, providing resources and strategies to overcome financial obstacles, prioritize self-care, and develop a holistic approach to your financial plan.

This subchapter will equip you with the tools and knowledge necessary to develop a comprehensive financial plan, whether amid a midlife crisis or simply seeking financial stability during a career change. By budgeting, saving, and investing for the future, you can confidently navigate this midlife journey, secure your financial freedom, and embrace the possibilities.

Exploring Entrepreneurship: Starting a Business or Side hustle.

In today's rapidly changing world, embarking on a new career path or starting a business in your 40s and beyond can be exciting and daunting. The need for financial freedom, retirement concerns, and the desire for self-discovery often converge during this stage of life, leading many men and women to consider entrepreneurship a viable option. This subchapter aims to guide individuals through exploring entrepreneurship and starting a business or side gig during the midlife years.

For those who have spent their entire lives in the public sector, retail, tourism, or health industries, transitioning into entrepreneurship may seem unfamiliar. However, this is the perfect time to harness your years of experience and expertise and turn them into a successful venture.

From identifying your passions and skills to conducting market research and creating a business plan, this subchapter will provide step-by-step guidance to help you navigate the entrepreneurial landscape.

One of the critical concerns during midlife is financial stability. Starting a business or side hustle can provide an additional source of income and offer the potential for long-term financial security. By exploring different business models, such as consulting, freelancing, or creating an online platform, you can leverage your existing knowledge and skills to create a sustainable and profitable business.

Moreover, midlife is often associated with health and wellness concerns. This subchapter will delve into the health and wellness entrepreneurship niche, highlighting opportunities in areas such as yoga, holistic health coaching, or wellness retreats. By combining your passion for wellness with the desire for financial independence, you can create a business that supports your well-being and helps others achieve a healthier and happier lifestyle.

We will address unique challenges and opportunities during midlife crises and self-discovery. From managing the fear of failure to embracing the freedom of exploring new skills and passions, entrepreneurship can be a transformative journey of self-discovery and personal growth.

In conclusion, "Exploring Entrepreneurship: Starting a Business or Side Hustle" is a comprehensive guide tailored to men and women over 40 who are seeking a career change, financial freedom, and self-discovery. Whether you are a public sector worker, retail employee, tourism professional, or health enthusiast, this subchapter will equip you with the knowledge and tools to embark on a successful entrepreneurial journey during your midlife.

Seeking Professional Help: Financial Advisors and Resources for Midlife Crisis

Midlife can be challenging, filled with uncertainty and a desire for change. As men and women enter their 40s and beyond, they often experience what is commonly known as a midlife crisis. A deep introspection and a search for self-discovery, career change, and financial freedom mark this period. However, tackling these concerns can be overwhelming without the guidance of a financial advisor and access to the right resources.

Financial advisors are crucial in helping individuals navigate the complex world of finances during a midlife crisis. These professionals have the expertise and knowledge to assess your financial situation, provide valuable advice, and create a customized plan to ensure long-term financial stability. They can help you set realistic goals, manage debts, invest wisely, and plan for retirement. For those in the public sector, retail, tourism, or health industries, specific considerations may be when seeking financial advice. Public sector workers often have unique retirement plans and benefits that require careful analysis. Retail and tourism workers may face uncertainties in their industries, making planning for career transitions and financial security essential.

Health professionals may have high levels of student debt or the desire to transition to a different field altogether. A financial advisor specializing in these areas can provide tailored guidance to address these concerns effectively.

In addition to seeking professional help, numerous resources are available to support individuals going through a midlife crisis. These resources can help you gain new skills, explore alternative career paths, and enhance your well-being. For example, if you are interested in health and wellness, you may find yoga classes or wellness retreats beneficial. These activities not only promote self-care but can also open doors to new opportunities and connections.

Remember, a midlife crisis can be an opportunity for self-discovery and personal growth. By seeking professional help from a financial advisor and utilizing the available resources, you can confidently navigate this phase's complexities. Take charge of your financial future, explore new career paths, and prioritize your health and well-being. The midlife journey may be challenging, but with the proper support, you can find your way to financial stability, career fulfilment, and a brighter future.

Chapter 4: Health and Wellness: Prioritising Self-Care and Wellbeing

Assessing Your Physical Health: Understanding the Impact of Midlife Crisis

In life's journey, reaching middle age can be a tumultuous period filled with many emotions, experiences, and challenges. One aspect that often takes a toll during this time is physical health. In this subchapter, we delve into the impact of midlife crisis on your physical well-being and why assessing and prioritising your health during this transformative phase is crucial.

For both men and women in their 40s and beyond, the midlife crisis can manifest in various ways. Career change, financial concerns, retirement worries, or a desire for self-discovery may trigger it. Regardless of the catalyst, it is essential to recognize how these factors can influence your physical health.

Financial instability, a common feature of midlife crisis, can lead to stress, anxiety, and even depression. These emotions can affect your physical well-being, affecting sleep patterns, appetite, and overall energy levels. Recognizing the impact of financial concerns on your health is the first step towards finding solutions and regaining control over your physical well-being.

Similarly, career change and retirement concerns can create uncertainty and instability. This transition often comes with added pressures and responsibilities, neglecting one's health. However, prioritizing your physical well-being is essential during this time, as it can help you navigate these changes with greater resilience and adaptability.

Engaging in activities that promote health and wellness becomes even more crucial during a midlife crisis. Exploring new skills, such as yoga or other forms of exercise, can improve your physical fitness and provide a much-needed outlet for stress and anxiety. It can also foster a sense of self-discovery and empowerment, helping you navigate the challenges of this phase with renewed vigour.

To honestly assess your physical health during a midlife crisis, it is imperative to take a comprehensive approach. It may include regular check-ups with healthcare professionals, maintaining a balanced diet, exercising regularly, and adopting stress management techniques.

By addressing your physical health needs, you can better equip yourself to navigate the complexities of midlife crisis and emerge on the other side with a stronger, healthier, and more resilient self.

In conclusion, understanding the impact of a midlife crisis on your physical health is crucial for men and women over 40 going through career changes, financial concerns, and retirement worries. By prioritizing your physical well-being, exploring new skills, and engaging in activities that promote health and wellness, you can successfully navigate the midlife maze and emerge with newfound strength, resilience, and self-discovery.

Ageing symptoms beyond your control

Menopause is a natural biological process that marks the end of a woman's reproductive years. It is defined as the point in time when a woman has not had a menstrual period for 12 consecutive months. Menopause typically occurs between 45 and 55, with the average age being 51. During menopause, a woman's body produces less oestrogen and progesterone, hormones that regulate menstruation. This decrease in hormone production can cause a range of symptoms, including hot flashes, night sweats, vaginal dryness, mood changes, and difficulty sleeping.

On the other hand, the term "male menopause" is sometimes used to describe age-related changes in male hormone levels. However, this term is misleading because it suggests that men experience a well-defined period of hormonal change similar to what women experience during menopause. In reality, hormone changes in men occur gradually over many years. They are not necessarily associated with specific symptoms or health problems.

Some men experience physical and emotional changes as they age, similar to those experienced by women during menopause. These changes may include decreased energy levels, reduced muscle mass, increased body fat, decreased sex drive, and mood changes. However, these changes are not necessarily caused by decreased hormone levels and may be related to other factors, such as lifestyle choices or underlying health conditions.

There are several self-help measures that both men and women can take to manage the symptoms of menopause and maintain good health as they age. These include:

- Eating a healthy diet: A diet rich in fruits, vegetables, whole grains, lean protein, and healthy fats can help maintain overall health and reduce the risk of chronic diseases such as heart disease and diabetes.
- Staying physically active: Regular physical activity can help maintain muscle mass, improve cardiovascular health, and reduce the risk of chronic diseases. It can also improve mood and sleep quality.
- Getting enough sleep: Good sleep hygiene is important for overall health and can help reduce the severity of menopausal symptoms such as hot flashes and mood changes.
- Managing stress: Stress can exacerbate menopausal symptoms and increase the risk of chronic diseases. Techniques such as deep breathing, meditation, or yoga can help manage stress levels.
- Avoiding triggers: Certain triggers such as caffeine, alcohol, and spicy foods can worsen hot flashes and other menopausal symptoms. Avoiding these triggers or consuming them in moderation may help reduce symptoms.

In summary, while menopause is a well-defined biological process in women, the concept of "male menopause" is not well-supported by scientific evidence. Both men and women can experience physical and emotional changes as they age that may be related to hormonal changes or other factors. Several self-help measures can help manage these changes and maintain good health during middle-age.

Embracing Healthy Habits: Nutrition, Exercise, and Self-Care Practices to keep your internal fat low and be healthier to avoid aging illnesses like heart conditions and diabetes.

Introduction: In our fast-paced modern world, finding time for self-care and maintaining a healthy lifestyle can often take a backseat, especially for individuals navigating the challenges of midlife. However, it is crucial to prioritize our well-being during this transformative phase of life. By embracing healthy habits such as proper nutrition, regular exercise, and self-care practices, we can keep our internal fat low and reduce the risk of ageing illnesses like heart conditions and diabetes. In this subchapter, we will explore the essential strategies to help men and women over 40 embrace a healthier lifestyle and confidently navigate the midlife journey.

Nutrition: Proper nutrition forms the foundation of a healthy lifestyle. As we age, our bodies undergo various changes, and it becomes even more important to nourish ourselves with nutrient-dense foods. This subchapter will provide valuable insights into developing a balanced diet, incorporating essential nutrients, and making healthier choices. We will explore the benefits of including whole grains, lean proteins, fruits, and vegetables in our daily meals while addressing common challenges such as managing portion sizes and controlling cravings.

Superfoods are nutrient-rich foods with numerous health benefits, especially for middle-aged individuals. As we age, it becomes increasingly more difficult to combat chronic diseases, maintain a healthy metabolism, and keep belly fat at bay. Adding specific superfoods to your diet can equip your body with the cancer-fighting, wrinkle-smoothing, and metabolism-revving vitamins and nutrients it needs to help you look and feel young and vibrant 1.

Some examples of superfoods that are beneficial for middle-aged individuals include wild salmon, which is rich in vitamin D3 and lean protein; plant-based milk, which can be easier to digest than dairy milk; chia seeds, which are a good source of omega-3 fatty acids; kimchi, which can help balance gut bacteria; and raspberries, which are high in fibre.

Superfood powders are a convenient way to boost nutrients in your diet. These powders are made from dried and ground superfoods, such as fruits, vegetables, and other plant-based foods, specifically chosen for their health benefits. Some popular superfood powders include moringa, acai, maca, chlorella, baobab, and spirulina.

Superfood powders can be easily added to smoothies and juices or sprinkled on top of foods like yoghurt or oatmeal. They provide a concentrated source of vitamins, minerals, antioxidants, and other beneficial compounds that can support overall health and well-being.

It's important to note that while superfood powders can be a convenient way to add more nutrients to your diet, they should not be relied upon as the sole source of nutrition.

Incorporating these superfoods into your diet can help support overall health and reduce the risk of age-related health conditions. It's important to remember that no single food can provide all the nutrients your body needs. Hence, eating a varied and balanced diet with a wide range of nutrient-rich foods is essential.

Exercise: Regular physical activity is crucial for maintaining optimal health and reducing the risk of age-related illnesses. With busy schedules and demanding careers, finding time for exercise may seem challenging. However, by incorporating simple activities, such as walking, yoga, or strength training, into our daily routine, we can reap significant health benefits. This subchapter will discuss various exercise options suitable for individuals in different professions and provide practical tips for establishing an exercise routine that fits seamlessly into our lives.

Addressing Mental Health: Managing Stress, Anxiety, and Depression with and without your doctor

In today's fast-paced world, it's common for men and women in their 40s and beyond to experience stress, anxiety, and depression. The pressures of career change, financial concerns, retirement worries, and the demands of the public sector worker, retail, tourism, and health industries can take a toll on our mental well-being. However, it's important to remember that you are not alone in this journey. This subchapter aims to provide practical tips and strategies to address your mental health concerns, whether you seek professional help or manage them on your own.

When managing stress, anxiety, and depression, one option is to consult with your doctor. They can diagnose properly, offer medication, and refer you to a mental health professional. Seeking professional help can be beneficial, as they have the expertise to guide you through your mental health journey. Additionally, they can help you explore coping mechanisms, such as cognitive-behavioural therapy or mindfulness techniques, to manage your symptoms effectively.

However, not everyone may have healthcare access or prefer to address their mental health concerns independently. In such cases, various self-help strategies can effectively manage stress, anxiety, and depression. One powerful tool is self-reflection and self-discovery. Understanding your triggers and identifying the root causes of your mental health concerns can help you develop personalized coping strategies. This can include setting boundaries, practising self-care, and engaging in activities that bring you joy and fulfilment, such as yoga or learning new skills.

Finding a support network is crucial, especially during times of midlife crisis. Surround yourself with friends, family, or like-minded individuals who understand and can empathise with your experiences. They can provide: Emotional support and guidance. Helping you navigate the challenges of career changes. Financial instability. Health concerns.

Lastly, prioritise your overall well-being. Maintain a healthy lifestyle by incorporating regular exercise, a balanced diet, and enough sleep into your routine. Additionally, consider stress management techniques, such as meditation or deep breathing exercises, to help alleviate anxiety and promote a sense of calm.

Remember, addressing mental health concerns is a personal journey; there is no one-size-fits-all approach. Whether you seek professional help or manage your mental health independently, the key is prioritising self-care, seeking support, and being open to exploring different strategies to find what works best for you. By doing so, you can navigate the midlife journey with resilience and ultimately achieve the sense of fulfilment, financial freedom, and overall well-being you deserve.

Is taking pills the only option for mental illness or can self help methods work

In today's fast-paced and demanding world, it is not uncommon for individuals to experience mental health challenges at some point. Whether it's stress, anxiety, or depression, these conditions can significantly impact our overall well-being and quality of life. However, Is taking pills the only solution, or can self-help methods provide relief?

While medication can be crucial in managing mental illness, it is not the only option available. Many individuals have successfully utilised self-help methods to improve their mental health and well-being.

One such self-help method that has gained popularity is mindfulness and meditation. These practices involve focusing on the present moment and cultivating a sense of calm and awareness. Research has shown that regular meditation can reduce stress, anxiety, and even symptoms of depression. It can also improve sleep patterns and enhance overall mental clarity.

Another effective self-help method is exercise. Regular physical activity, such as yoga or walking, has been proven to release endorphins, also known as "feel-good" hormones. These endorphins can alleviate symptoms of depression and anxiety, boost self-esteem, and improve overall mood.

Additionally, healthy lifestyle habits can significantly impact mental health, including eating a balanced diet, getting enough sleep, and avoiding excessive alcohol or drug consumption. Such practices can provide a solid foundation for managing mental health challenges and promoting well-being.

Of course, it is essential to note that self-help methods may not work for everyone, and seeking professional help is crucial in some instances. Mental health professionals can provide invaluable support and guidance. They may recommend a combination of therapy and medication for optimal results.

In conclusion, while medication can effectively manage mental illness, it is not the only option. Self-help methods such as mindfulness, exercise, and healthy lifestyle habits can also significantly improve mental health and well-being. Finding what works best for you and seeking professional help when needed is essential. Individuals can navigate the midlife maze with greater resilience and self-discovery by taking a holistic approach to mental health.

Exploring Alternative Therapies: Yoga, Meditation, and Mindfulness

In the fast-paced, ever-changing world we live in today, many of us find ourselves at a crossroads in our lives, particularly those in their 40s and beyond. The pressures of career change, financial concerns, and worries about retirement can all contribute to a midlife crisis. But what if there were alternative therapies that could help navigate this turbulent period with grace and self-discovery? Enter yoga, meditation, and mindfulness – practices that have gained popularity recently due to their numerous mental, physical, and emotional benefits.

The concept of a midlife crisis can be overwhelming for men and women in their 40s and beyond. However, it is essential to remember that this period can also be a time of self-discovery and personal growth. Alternative therapies such as yoga, meditation, and mindfulness can provide the tools to navigate these challenges and find inner peace.

Yoga, combining physical postures, breathwork, and meditation, offers a holistic approach to health and well-being. Through regular practice, individuals can improve their strength, flexibility, and balance while reducing stress and anxiety. Additionally, yoga can help alleviate common ailments associated with ageing, such as chronic pain and arthritis, making it an ideal practice for those in their middle years.

Conversely, meditation focuses on quieting the mind and cultivating a sense of inner calm. We can gain insight into our emotions and reactions by taking time each day to sit in stillness and observe our thoughts. This self-awareness can be transformative, allowing us to make conscious choices and break free from old patterns that no longer serve us.

Mindfulness, often practised with meditation, involves bringing our attention to the present moment. It encourages us to fully engage with our experiences, whether they are positive or negative, without judgment. By cultivating this non-judgmental awareness, we can better manage stress, improve our relationships, and find greater satisfaction in our daily lives.

By incorporating yoga, meditation, and mindfulness into their routines, individuals can reduce stress, improve focus and productivity, and enhance their overall well-being. Moreover, these practices can also provide an opportunity to explore new skills and passions, leading to potential career changes or financial freedom.

In conclusion, exploring alternative therapies such as yoga, meditation, and mindfulness can be transformative for men and women in their 40s and beyond. By embracing these practices, individuals can navigate the challenges of a midlife crisis with grace, discover new career possibilities, achieve financial stability, and prioritize their health and well-being. So, if you find yourself at a crossroads, why not embark on this path of self-discovery and see where it leads? Your future self will thank you.

Chapter 5: Acquiring New Skills: Upskilling and Adapting to the Changing Job Market

Identifying In-Demand Skills: Researching Job Market Trends

In today's rapidly evolving job market, staying ahead of the curve is essential for anyone considering a career change, especially those in their 40s and beyond. As you navigate the midlife journey and seek new opportunities, it is crucial to identify the in-demand skills that will make you stand out from the competition. Researching job market trends can provide valuable insights into emerging industries, changing needs, and skill requirements. This subchapter will help you identify these skills and make informed decisions about your career path.

Understanding job market trends requires a systematic approach. Begin by exploring various sectors and industries that align with your interests, experience, and goals. For our audience, we'll specifically focus on industries such as public sector work, retail, tourism, and health, as these are areas where many midlife career changers find new opportunities.

Start your research by leveraging online resources, industry reports, and government websites that provide information on job growth, salary ranges, and emerging skill demands. For example, suppose you are considering a career in the public sector. In that case, skills in data analysis, project management, or digital transformation are increasingly sought after.

Next, consider the niche areas that resonate with your midlife concerns. For instance, if you are experiencing a midlife crisis and seeking self-discovery, industries related to personal development, coaching, or counselling could be a good fit. Alternatively, if financial instability is a primary concern, exploring skills in financial planning, entrepreneurship, or digital marketing could provide more stability and opportunities for growth.

Health and wellness have become increasingly important in recent years, and this trend is expected to continue. If you are passionate about health and wellness, consider acquiring skills in nutrition, fitness training, holistic healing practices, or even yoga instruction. These skills can open doors to various opportunities, from working in wellness retreats to starting your own business.

As you research, pay attention to the skills consistently appearing across different industries. These transferable skills, such as communication, leadership, problem-solving, adaptability, and technological proficiency, are highly valued by employers regardless of the sector. Focusing on developing and highlighting these skills will enhance your marketability and increase your chances of success during a career transition.

By investing time in researching the job market trends, you will gain a clear understanding of the skills and qualifications that are currently in high demand. Armed with this knowledge, you can confidently pursue new career paths that align with your interests, provide financial stability, and offer a sense of fulfilment during this transformative phase of life. Remember, there is always time to learn something new and embark on a rewarding journey towards personal and professional growth.

Pursuing Continuing Education: Online digital Courses, and Certification Programs

In our ever-evolving world, it is essential to keep our skills up to date and stay ahead of the game. This rings especially true for men and women in their 40s and beyond, who may be contemplating a career change, seeking financial freedom, or grappling with concerns about retirement. Suppose you are in the public sector, retail, tourism, or health industries. In that case, you might be wondering how to acquire new skills to navigate the challenges of midlife.

Enter online digital courses and certification programs, the perfect solution for those seeking personal and professional growth in their middle age. These platforms offer many opportunities for individuals experiencing a midlife crisis, helping them embark on a journey of self-discovery, financial stability, and improved health and wellness.

Midlife is often associated with a period of reflection and reassessment, where individuals question their life choices and direction. Online digital courses can be a transformative tool during this phase, providing the chance to explore new interests, learn about different industries, and discover untapped potential. Whether you've always dreamt of starting a yoga studio, delving into the world of technology, or becoming a healthcare professional, these courses offer a gateway to turn your aspirations into reality.

Moreover, financial freedom is a common concern for those approaching midlife. Online courses and certification programs can provide the necessary tools and knowledge to embark on a new career path, potentially leading to more excellent financial stability. By acquiring new skills and staying updated with industry trends, you can position yourself as a valuable asset in the job market, opening doors to exciting opportunities and higher earning potential.

Health and wellness are also crucial aspects of midlife. You can explore various wellness practices through online digital courses, such as yoga, meditation, nutrition, and holistic healing. Not only will you enhance your well-being, but you may also discover a newfound passion for helping others improve their health. This could lead to a fulfilling and rewarding second career in the booming health and wellness industry.

In summary, online digital courses and certification programs offer a lifeline for men and women in their 40s and beyond, navigating the complexities of midlife. Whether experiencing a midlife crisis, seeking self-discovery, financial stability, or improved health and wellness, these platforms provide many opportunities to acquire new skills and transform your life. Embrace the power of lifelong learning and embark on a personal and professional growth journey – the possibilities are endless!

Leveraging Transferable Skills: Applying Existing Knowledge to New Opportunities and learn new digital skills.

In today's rapidly changing job market, career transitions have become common, especially for those in their 40s and beyond. Midlife A True Journey is here to guide you through this challenging phase, offering practical advice and inspiration to help you navigate the often confusing world of midlife career change.

One of the key strategies we explore in this book is the concept of leveraging transferable skills. As a seasoned professional, you have undoubtedly acquired a wealth of knowledge and expertise in your current field. These skills can be precious in opening up new opportunities, even in industries that may seem vastly different from your previous experience.

By identifying your core competencies, you can highlight these transferable skills and demonstrate to potential employers how they can be applied to new contexts. For example, suppose you are a public sector worker with excellent communication and problem-solving skills. These qualities can be invaluable in customer service roles within the retail or tourism industries.

In addition to leveraging your existing knowledge, it is vital to recognize the importance of acquiring new digital skills. The world has become increasingly reliant on technology, and navigating digital platforms and tools has become essential for career success. Whether you are interested in pursuing a career in health and wellness or exploring opportunities in the yoga industry, having a solid foundation in digital skills can significantly enhance your prospects.

The Midlife journey provides practical guidance on acquiring these new digital skills. From online courses to workshops and networking events, we explore various avenues for learning and development. We also delve into the benefits of embracing technology, such as working remotely, starting an online business, or even reaching a global audience with your expertise.

Whether going through a midlife crisis, seeking self-discovery, or facing financial instability, this subchapter offers invaluable insights tailored to your needs. By leveraging your transferable skills and embracing digital learning opportunities, you can confidently navigate the midlife journey, find new career paths, and achieve the financial freedom and fulfilment you desire.

Remember, your age and experience should be seen as assets, not obstacles. With the right mindset and strategies, you can embark on a new chapter of your professional life and discover a world of exciting possibilities.

How easy is it to start a business in digital marketing, affiliate marketing is a great place to start and what it is.

In this digital age, starting a business in digital marketing has become increasingly accessible and lucrative. Whether you are a man or woman in your 40s or beyond, considering a career change, or concerned about retirement and financial freedom, digital marketing offers an excellent opportunity for self-discovery and financial stability.

Affiliate marketing is one of the easiest and most effective ways to jumpstart your digital marketing journey. Affiliate marketing is a performance-based marketing model where individuals promote the products or services of others and earn a commission for every sale made through their referrals. It is an ideal starting point for those looking to venture into digital marketing with limited resources and experience.

The beauty of affiliate marketing lies in its simplicity. With minimal upfront investment, you can leverage the power of the internet and earn passive income. Unlike traditional businesses that require substantial capital, inventory, and overhead costs, affiliate marketing allows you to work from home.

To get started, you need to select a niche that aligns with your interests, expertise, and the target audience you want to reach. Consider the niches of a midlife crisis, self-discovery, financial instability, and health and wellness, which resonate with individuals in their 40s and beyond. For example, if you have a background in retail or tourism, you could explore affiliate partnerships with travel agencies or online retailers specializing in midlife-related products.

Once you have chosen a niche, you can create a website or blog to share valuable content and promote relevant products or services through affiliate links. By producing high-quality content that addresses the concerns and interests of your target audience, you can build trust and establish yourself as an authority in your chosen niche.

You promote your affiliate links through various channels, including social media platforms, email marketing, and search engine optimization. The key is to develop a comprehensive digital marketing strategy that leverages these channels to drive traffic to your website and convert visitors into customers.

While starting a business in digital marketing may seem daunting at first, affiliate marketing offers a low-risk and high-reward opportunity for individuals in their 40s and beyond. With dedication, continuous learning, and a strategic approach, you can build a successful online business that provides financial freedom and a fulfilling career amid a midlife crisis.

Networking and Mentorship: Building Connections in Your Desired Field

In today's rapidly changing job market, building a solid network and finding a mentor is essential to navigating a successful career change in your 40s and beyond. Whether looking for a change in profession, seeking financial freedom, or concerned about retirement, networking and mentorship can provide invaluable support, guidance, and opportunities.

For men and women in their midlife, networking might seem intimidating or unfamiliar. However, the right strategies and mindset can become an empowering tool to open doors and create new possibilities. Regardless of your background or industry, cultivating connections can lead to career growth, job openings, and even unexpected ventures.

Networking is about more than just attending industry events and collecting business cards. It's about building genuine relationships with like-minded individuals who share your interests and aspirations. By joining professional associations, attending seminars, and participating in online communities, you can connect with others who have gone through similar career transitions or possess expertise in your desired field.

But don't limit yourself to networking within your industry alone. Consider reaching out to individuals in related fields, as they may offer unique perspectives and potential collaboration opportunities. For example, a public sector worker interested in starting a retail business could benefit from connecting with professionals in the tourism or health sectors.

In addition to networking, finding a mentor can significantly accelerate your career change and self-discovery journey. A mentor is someone who has achieved success in your desired field and is willing to share their knowledge, experiences, and guidance with you. They can offer valuable insights, provide feedback on your ideas and plans, and offer support during challenging times.

To find a mentor: Start by identifying individuals who inspire you or whose achievements align with your goals. Reach out to them and express your admiration for their work, explaining why you believe their guidance would be valuable to you. Remember, mentors are often busy professionals, so respect their time and show genuine interest and commitment.

Finally, consider the importance of building a diverse and inclusive network. Seek out connections from different industries, backgrounds, and perspectives. This will broaden your horizons and enhance your problem-solving skills and creativity.

Networking and mentorship are potent tools for navigating the midlife journey of career change, financial freedom, retirement concerns, and personal growth. By actively engaging in these practices, you can build meaningful connections, gain valuable insights, and uncover new opportunities to propel you towards a fulfilling and prosperous future.

Chapter 6: Retirement Concerns: Planning for Financial Security and a Meaningful Future

Rethinking Retirement: Redefining the Concept in the Midlife Crisis Era

In our fast-paced, ever-evolving world, retirement has undergone a significant transformation. Gone are the days when retirement meant bidding farewell to work and embracing a life of leisure. Today, the midlife crisis era demands a revaluation of retirement, combining self-discovery, career change, and financial freedom.

For men and women over 40, the midlife crisis often brings about a sense of restlessness and a desire for change. It could be a perfect time to rethink retirement and redefine it as a period of self-discovery. Instead of viewing retirement as the end of a career, it may be an opportunity to explore new passions and interests. By embracing a career change, individuals can embark on a journey of self-discovery, finding fulfilment in new pursuits and reigniting their sense of purpose.

Financial freedom is another crucial aspect of redefining retirement. Many individuals in the midlife crisis era find themselves grappling with economic instability. However, with careful planning and the right mindset, it is possible to achieve financial freedom. By reassessing expenses, exploring new income streams, and investing wisely, individuals can secure their financial future and enjoy a fulfilling retirement.

This revised concept of retirement also addresses the concerns of public sector workers, retail employees, and those in the tourism and health industries. The midlife crisis can create unique challenges for individuals in these sectors, including burnout and a lack of fulfilment. By rethinking retirement, individuals in these fields can find new ways to utilize their skills and expertise, whether through consulting, teaching, or starting their businesses.

Furthermore, this new approach to retirement emphasises the importance of health and wellness. Midlife crisis and health often go hand in hand as individuals become more aware of prioritising their well-being. Retirement is an opportunity to focus on self-care, whether practising yoga, engaging in physical activity, or adopting healthier lifestyle choices. By prioritising health and wellness, individuals can navigate the midlife crisis era with resilience and vitality.

In conclusion, rethinking retirement in the midlife crisis era involves: Embracing self-discovery. Pursuing a career change. Attaining financial freedom. Prioritizing health and wellness. By adopting this new perspective, men and women over 40 can confidently navigate the journey of midlife, finding fulfilment and purpose in their later years.

Developing a Retirement Plan: Investing, Saving, and Budgeting for the Future

Introduction: As we navigate through our 40s and beyond, many of us find ourselves facing the prospect of retirement. This subchapter aims to provide valuable insights and guidance on developing a retirement plan that ensures financial stability and freedom during this crucial phase of life. Whether you are going through a midlife crisis, contemplating a career change, or want to secure your financial future, understanding the importance of investing, saving, and budgeting is essential.

Investing for the Future:
Investing can be a powerful tool for building wealth and ensuring a comfortable retirement. This section discusses various investment strategies, such as stocks, bonds, real estate, and mutual funds. We explore the concept of diversification and how it can help mitigate risks while maximizing returns. Additionally, we delve into the importance of seeking professional advice and staying informed about market trends to make well-informed investment decisions.

Saving for Retirement:

Saving is the foundation of any retirement plan. Whether you are a public sector worker, retail employee, tourism professional, or healthcare provider, this section provides practical tips on how to save effectively. We discuss the benefits of employer-sponsored retirement plans, such as 401(k)in the US or SIPP (Self-Invested Personal Pension) in the UK and other pension schemes, and emphasize the need to take advantage of these opportunities. Furthermore, we highlight the importance of setting realistic savings goals and establishing a disciplined approach to saving.

Budgeting for Financial Freedom:

Budgeting is a vital skill that helps individuals gain control over their finances. This section explores effective budgeting techniques that can contribute to long-term financial stability. We discuss creating a comprehensive budget, tracking expenses, and identifying areas where spending can be reduced. Additionally, we address the impact of lifestyle choices on retirement planning and offer practical suggestions for making sustainable changes.

Addressing Midlife Crisis Concerns:

For those experiencing a midlife crisis, this subchapter acknowledges the unique challenges that can arise in this phase. We discuss how a well-structured retirement plan can provide a sense of purpose and alleviate financial instability concerns. Moreover, we explore the role of self-discovery and personal growth in navigating through this transitional period, focusing on maintaining mental and physical well-being.

Conclusion:

Developing a retirement plan is critical to achieving financial freedom and a secure future. By investing wisely, saving diligently, and budgeting effectively, individuals in their 40s and beyond can lay a solid foundation for retirement. This subchapter provides valuable insights and practical advice tailored to the needs of men and women experiencing a midlife crisis, contemplating a career change, and seeking financial stability. It addresses concerns related to health and wellness, emphasizing the importance of self-discovery and personal growth throughout the journey towards retirement. With the proper knowledge and strategies, everyone can navigate the midlife journey and embark on a fulfilling and prosperous retirement journey.

What is the average government pension and will it be enough to live on when you retire?

As you approach your 40s and beyond, thoughts of retirement become more prevalent. After years of hard work and dedication, you want to ensure your golden years are comfortable and stress-free. But have you ever wondered what the average government pension is and if it will be enough to live on when you retire?

For many individuals, working in the public sector has perks, including the promise of a pension. However, the average government pension varies depending on salary, years of service, and the chosen retirement plan. While there is no one-size-fits-all answer, understanding the average figures can help you make informed decisions about your financial future.

Recent data indicates that the average government pension in the United States falls between $30,000 to $60,000 yearly. In the United Kingdom, the government state pension stands at £10,600 per year, with an average of £19,000 annually when complemented with workplace or other pension schemes. While these sums may appear significant, it is crucial to account for your lifestyle, inflation, and possible healthcare expenses. Furthermore, suppose you have dependents or outstanding debts. In that case, your pension may not be adequate to cover all your costs as you initially anticipated.

Financial freedom during retirement requires careful planning and consideration. It is crucial to evaluate your current expenses, future goals, and any additional sources of income if you find that your projected pension needs to meet your desired lifestyle, there are steps you can take to bridge the gap.

One option is to explore new skills and career opportunities that can provide supplemental income during retirement. It could involve starting a small business, freelancing, or working part-time. By diversifying your income streams, you can ensure a more comfortable retirement and mitigate any financial instability that may arise.

Another aspect to consider is your health and wellness. Midlife is a crucial time to focus on self-discovery, including caring for your physical and mental well-being. Engaging in activities such as yoga, meditation, or regular exercise can improve your quality of life and reduce healthcare costs in the long run.

While the average government pension can provide a foundation for retirement, more is needed. As you navigate your midlife years, it is essential to explore new career opportunities, prioritise your health and wellness, and develop a comprehensive financial plan that ensures your retirement concerns are addressed. By taking proactive steps now, you can achieve your desired financial freedom and embark on a fulfilling and stress-free retirement journey.

Exploring Retirement Options: Part-Time Work, Volunteering, and creating a passive online income

As we approach our 40s and beyond, retirement concerns start creeping into our minds. Leaving a long career and transitioning into a new phase of life can be exciting and overwhelming. It's a time for self-discovery, financial freedom, and choices that align with our passions and interests. In this subchapter, we will explore three retirement options that can help you navigate the midlife journey: part-time work, volunteerism, and creating a passive online income.

Part-Time Work:

For many individuals, completely retiring from work isn't the ideal solution. A part-time job offers a middle ground, allowing you to continue earning income while enjoying more flexibility and freedom. This option is particularly suitable for public sector workers, retail professionals, and those in the tourism industry who may still have valuable skills and knowledge to offer. Part-time work can provide a sense of purpose, social interaction, and the opportunity to explore new avenues.

Volunteering:

Retirement is the perfect time to give back to the community and make a positive impact. Engaging in volunteer work can be immensely fulfilling and rewarding. Whether it's working with a local charity, mentoring others, or contributing to environmental causes, you have countless opportunities to get involved. Volunteering allows you to make a difference and helps you develop new skills, expand your network, and find a renewed sense of purpose.

Creating a Passive Online Income:

The internet has opened up a world of possibilities for generating income from the comfort of your own home. Creating a passive online income is an excellent option for those seeking financial stability during retirement. Whether starting an e-commerce store, monetizing a blog, or becoming an affiliate marketer, the online world offers numerous avenues to explore. It provides the flexibility to work at your own pace, pursue your interests, and generate a steady income stream without being tied to a traditional job.

Furthermore, this subchapter will address the midlife crisis and self-discovery concerns, financial instability, and health and wellness during this transitional phase. We will discuss how each retirement option can contribute to personal growth, financial security, and well-being.

Ultimately, the key to navigating the midlife journey is to embrace change, explore new possibilities, and align your choices with your values and passions. By considering part-time work, volunteering, and creating a passive online income, you can embark on a fulfilling retirement journey that offers purpose, financial freedom, and a renewed focus on health and wellness.

Creating a Fulfilling Retirement: Balancing Leisure, Hobbies, and Personal Growth

Retirement is a significant milestone in life, representing the end of one's working years and the beginning of a new chapter filled with endless possibilities. However, the transition into retirement can be daunting for many individuals, especially those in their 40s and beyond who are undergoing a career change or grappling with financial concerns.

One of the key elements to creating a fulfilling retirement is finding a balance between leisure, hobbies, and personal growth. It is essential to recognize that retirement is not just about lounging on a beach or playing golf all day but rather an opportunity to explore new interests, develop new skills, and embark on a journey of self-discovery.

For those who have spent their entire careers in the public sector, retail, tourism, or health industries, retirement can be a chance to delve into new hobbies or pursue long-held passions. Whether taking up painting, learning a musical instrument, or exploring the world of photography, retirement offers the freedom to indulge in activities that bring joy and fulfilment.

Furthermore, retirement can also be a time for personal growth and self-improvement. Engaging in new experiences and challenges can help individuals maintain mental sharpness, boost self-confidence, and foster a sense of purpose. This could involve enrolling in a yoga class, learning a new language, or volunteering for a cause close to your heart. The possibilities are endless, and the journey is yours to shape.

However, it is also essential to consider the financial aspect of retirement. The book delves into strategies for achieving financial freedom, including effective budgeting, investment options, and creating multiple income streams. By addressing retirement concerns and developing a solid financial plan, individuals can pursue their passions without the added burden of economic instability.

This book also discusses the impact of retirement on health and wellness. A midlife crisis can often lead to neglecting one's well-being, both physically and mentally. Through insightful guidance, readers will learn the importance of maintaining a healthy lifestyle, including exercise, proper nutrition, and nurturing social connections.

In conclusion, retirement can be an exciting and fulfilling phase of life if approached with intention and balance. By embracing leisure, exploring new hobbies, fostering personal growth, and addressing financial and health concerns, individuals can gracefully navigate their midlife crisis and embark on a path of self-discovery and contentment. "Midlife A True Journey" offers the tools and guidance needed to create a satisfying and enriching retirement.

Chapter 7: Midlife Crisis in Different Professions: Challenges and Solutions for Public Sector Workers, Retail Employees, and Those who deal with the public

Midlife Crisis in the Public Sector: Navigating Bureaucracy and Seeking New Opportunities

Introduction:

In the fast-paced world of the public sector, a midlife crisis can be an overwhelming experience. Navigating bureaucracy and the desire for new opportunities can create a sense of restlessness and dissatisfaction. However, this stage of life also presents a unique opportunity for self-discovery, career change, and personal growth. In this subchapter, we will explore how individuals in the public sector can effectively navigate their midlife crisis, find financial freedom, prioritise health and wellness, and embark on a journey of self-discovery.

Navigating Bureaucracy:

The public sector is often associated with a rigid bureaucratic structure, making it challenging for individuals to break free from their routines and explore new possibilities. However, it is crucial to recognize that change is possible even within this system. By developing a strategic plan, building a solid professional network, and seeking opportunities for growth and advancement, individuals can navigate the bureaucratic maze and find new challenges that reignite their passion and purpose.

Seeking New Opportunities:

Midlife crises often arise from stagnation and the desire for new challenges. The key to overcoming this is identifying transferable skills and exploring alternative career paths. Many public sector workers possess valuable skills that could be transferrable in various industries such as retail, tourism, or health. By acquiring new skills and seeking opportunities outside their comfort zone, individuals can open doors to exciting new possibilities and find fulfilment in their work.

Financial Freedom and Retirement Concerns: Midlife crisis often brings about concerns about financial stability and retirement plans. It is crucial to take stock of one's financial situation and create a long-term strategy that aligns with personal goals.

Exploring options such as entrepreneurship, part-time work, or investment opportunities can provide the financial freedom to navigate this life phase comfortably.

Prioritising Health and Wellness:

A midlife crisis can take a toll on physical and mental health. It is essential to prioritise self-care and well-being during this period. Engaging in yoga, meditation, or hobbies promoting relaxation and reducing stress can significantly contribute to overall health and well-being. Taking proactive steps towards a healthy lifestyle can provide the energy and resilience to navigate challenges and embrace new opportunities.

Conclusion:

Midlife crisis in the public sector can seem daunting, but it is also an opportunity for growth and self-discovery. Individuals can successfully navigate this phase of life by navigating bureaucracy, seeking new opportunities, finding financial freedom, and prioritizing health and wellness. Remember, there is always time to change and find fulfilment in your career and personal life. Embrace the challenges, explore new possibilities, and embark on self-discovery and transformation. The midlife maze may be complex, but with the right mindset and determination, you can navigate it and emerge stronger than ever.

Transitioning from Retail to a New Career: Transferable Skills and Job Market Analysis

In today's fast-paced and ever-evolving job market, many individuals find themselves at a crossroads in their careers, especially those in their 40s and beyond. One common scenario is transitioning from a career in retail to a new path that aligns with their passions, financial goals, and personal growth. This subchapter aims to guide men and women through this process, providing valuable insights on transferable skills and a comprehensive job market analysis.

When embarking on a career change, it is crucial to identify the transferable skills acquired during your time in retail. Despite the differences between industries, specific skills are universally applicable and highly sought after by employers. Communication, customer service, problem-solving, time management, teamwork, and adaptability are just a few examples of skills usable in various roles. Recognising and leveraging these skills can significantly enhance your chances of success in a new career.

However, before diving headfirst into a new field, conducting a thorough job market analysis is essential. Understanding the demand, growth potential, and opportunities within different industries will enable you to make informed decisions about your career transition. This analysis should consider salary trends, job availability, required qualifications, and prospects. By aligning your skills and interests with a promising industry, you will increase your chances of finding financial freedom, job satisfaction, and long-term stability.

This subchapter is particularly relevant to public sector workers, retail professionals, tourism industry professionals, and individuals interested in health and wellness. It addresses this audience's unique challenges and concerns, including retirement worries and the need for new skills to stay competitive in the job market. Additionally, it explores the connection between midlife crisis and self-discovery, financial instability, and health and wellness.

Whether considering a complete career overhaul or a gradual transition, this subchapter provides practical strategies, real-life examples, and expert advice to support you through this transformative journey. By focusing on transferable skills and conducting a comprehensive job market analysis, you can confidently navigate the midlife journey, embracing new opportunities and finding fulfilment in a new career that aligns with your passions and goals.

Surviving Midlife Crisis in a job outside the 9-5 Industry: Reinventing Yourself in a Changing Market

Many individuals face a midlife crisis in today's fast-paced and ever-changing job market. This stage of life, typically occurring in one's 40s and beyond, brings unique challenges and concerns. However, it is essential to remember that this period can also be an opportunity for self-discovery, career change, and financial freedom.

For those who have spent their careers in the public sector, retail, tourism, or health industries, leaving the comfort of a stable 9-5 job can be intimidating. However, by embracing the changing market and reinventing yourself, you can navigate this midlife crisis with grace and resilience.

One key aspect of surviving a midlife crisis is recognizing the need for change and embracing new skills. The job market is constantly evolving, and staying ahead of the curve is essential. Consider exploring new industries or sectors that align with your passions and interests. For example, you have always been intrigued by the yoga and wellness world. Why not consider becoming a certified yoga instructor? This allows you to pursue a career that brings you joy and caters to the niche of midlife crisis and health and wellness.

Financial concerns often accompany midlife crisis, especially when transitioning from a stable job to a new industry. It is crucial to plan and prepare for this change. Take the time to assess your financial situation and explore opportunities for financial freedom. This might include saving money, investing wisely, or even seeking financial advice from professionals specialising in midlife crises and economic instability.

Another critical aspect of surviving a midlife crisis is self-discovery. Midlife offers a unique opportunity to reflect on your values, desires, and aspirations. Take the time to assess your skills, strengths, and weaknesses. This self-reflection will help guide you towards a career that brings financial stability and aligns with your true passions and purpose.

In conclusion, navigating a midlife crisis in a changing job market can be daunting. Still, it is also a chance for growth and self-discovery. By embracing new skills, planning for financial stability, and exploring new career opportunities, you can reinvent yourself and find fulfilment outside the 9-5 industry. Remember, midlife is not the end; it is a new beginning. Embrace the journey and seize the opportunity to create your desired life.

From Retail Manager to Successful Entrepreneur: My Journey Through Midlife Crisis

As a middle-aged manager in the retail industry, I found myself at a crossroads. Despite my successful career, I lacked fulfilment and yearned for something more. Recognising the need for change, I pursued my passion for writing. With relentless determination and hard work, I published my first short book, which became instantly popular. This unexpected success of this book encouraged me into the world of literature and got the bug to write a second.

With an eye on the digital age, I realised the potential of digital marketing and its ability to reach a global audience. I honed my skills by attending online workshops and gaining expertise in this emerging field. Leveraging my newfound knowledge, I established a brand that quickly gained recognition for its innovative strategies and exceptional results. This venture not only provided financial stability but also allowed me to explore my creativity and entrepreneurial spirit.

My incredible journey deeply inspired me, motivating me to delve into entrepreneurship. With my extensive retail industry knowledge, I embarked on a mission to create a coaching business that specialises in health and wellness products. Thanks to my hard work and dedication, my e-commerce platform has become a huge success, featuring a carefully curated selection of products that cater to the ever-growing demand for holistic well-being. People flock to my business as it has become the ideal destination for anyone seeking self-care solutions to promote a healthy lifestyle and a more fulfilling midlife experience.

Through these diverse experiences, I not only achieved financial freedom but also discovered a newfound sense of purpose and fulfilment. My story resonates with individuals facing midlife crises, reminding them that it is never too late to redefine their lives and pursue their passions. My journey offers inspiration and practical insights into how one can navigate the challenges of a midlife crisis and emerge stronger, both personally and professionally.

Furthermore, my experience highlights the importance of acquiring new skills in today's rapidly evolving world. My transition from a retail manager to a successful author, digital marketer, and business owner underscores the value of continuous learning and adaptability. Finally, my journey aligns with the niche of midlife crisis and health and wellness, as my focus on holistic well-being and yoga as a means of self-discovery and personal growth played a pivotal role in my transformation.

In conclusion, my success story inspires anyone navigating a midlife crisis, contemplating a career change, or seeking financial freedom in their 40s and beyond. My journey exemplifies the power of self-discovery, resilience, and adaptability, offering practical lessons and insights to the audience of "Midlife A True Journey".

No technical skill can be learnt and is essential as the world is changing, how Ai is transforming the world it is today and jobs are going in certain industries.

The Impact of AI on Midlife Career Change and Self-Discovery:

In today's rapidly evolving world, the advent of Artificial Intelligence (AI) is transforming industries and reshaping the job market. This subchapter explores the profound effects of AI on individuals going through a midlife career change, particularly those in their 40s and beyond.

As men and women in middle age embark on a career change journey, the need to adapt and acquire new skills becomes crucial. However, it is essential to note that no technical skill can be considered immutable or indispensable. The world is changing at an unprecedented pace, and what is relevant today may become outdated tomorrow. This realisation can be daunting but also presents an opportunity for personal growth, self-discovery, and embracing new possibilities.

With its ability to automate tasks and streamline processes, AI has become a game-changer across various industries. Sectors such as public administration, retail, tourism, and healthcare are witnessing significant transformations due to the integration of AI technologies.

While this may lead to concerns about job security, it also opens up avenues for career reinvention and financial freedom for those willing to adapt.

For individuals experiencing a midlife crisis, this technological shift can catalyze self-discovery. It prompts them to reflect on their passions, interests, and values and encourages exploration of alternative career paths. By embracing new skills and honing their abilities, individuals can navigate the changing job landscape and find fulfilling opportunities in emerging industries influenced by AI.

Moreover, the subchapter addresses the financial instability often associated with midlife crises. It highlights the potential of AI to create new jobs and industries, providing opportunities for individuals seeking financial stability and independence. By acquiring skills in AI-related fields, such as data analysis, machine learning, or programming, midlife career changers can position themselves for success in the rapidly growing AI-driven job market.

In conclusion, the transformative power of AI must be addressed in today's world. Individuals experiencing a midlife crisis can embark on self-discovery, financial stability, and enhanced well-being by recognising the changing landscape, embracing new skills, and leveraging AI technologies. This subchapter guides those seeking to navigate the midlife journey and thrive in an AI-driven future.

Chapter 8: Embracing the Journey: Finding Confidence, Purpose, and Happiness in Midlife Crisis

Building Self-Confidence: Overcoming Doubts and Embracing Change

In life's journey, reaching midlife often brings about a period of self-reflection and introspection. During this time, many of us begin to question our choices, careers, and even our abilities. Doubts can creep in, and we may find ourselves at a crossroads, unsure how to navigate the path ahead. However, this is also a time of immense opportunity for personal growth and self-discovery. This subchapter will explore the importance of building self-confidence, overcoming doubts, and embracing change during midlife.

Career change and financial freedom are common concerns for men and women in their 40s and beyond. Many may feel trapped in unfulfilling jobs or want to explore new opportunities but fear leaping. Self-confidence plays a crucial role in this process. By recognising your strengths, skills, and unique experiences, you can believe in your ability to succeed in a new career or venture.

Retirement concerns often loom large during midlife, particularly for those in the public sector, retail, tourism, and health industries. Building self-confidence can help alleviate fears about financial stability and retirement planning. By embracing change and acquiring new skills, you can open doors to new career possibilities or even start a side business to supplement your income.

Midlife crisis is often associated with a sense of lost purpose and identity. However, this can also be a transformative phase for self-discovery. By challenging limiting beliefs and embracing change, you can embark on a journey of self-exploration that leads to greater fulfilment and happiness. Health and wellness are essential aspects of midlife crisis and self-discovery. Engaging in activities like yoga can improve physical well-being, boost self-confidence, and provide a sense of inner peace.

In conclusion, midlife is a time of transition and self-discovery. By building self-confidence, overcoming doubts, and embracing change, you can navigate this phase with greater ease and grace. Whether considering a career change, financial freedom, or exploring new skills and interests, remember that it is always possible to reinvent yourself and create a life that aligns with your true passions and values. Embrace the opportunities that come your way and trust in your abilities. The journey may not always be easy, but with self-confidence as your anchor, you have the power to create a fulfilling and purposeful life in your 40s and beyond.

Self belief through Midlife

Self-belief is a fundamental quality that determines success in every aspect of life. It is the confidence you have in yourself, your abilities, and your decisions, and it plays a crucial role in shaping your approach to life and the challenges that come your way. Without self-belief, you are more likely to shy away from risks, doubt your decisions, and give up easily when faced with obstacles.

On the other hand, having self-belief sets you up for success. It enables you to approach challenges with a positive mindset and the conviction that you can overcome them. Self-belief makes you more likely to take calculated risks, persist in the face of failure and adversity, and remain committed to your goals even when the going gets tough.

One reason why self-belief is so important is that it allows you to tap into your full potential. When you believe in yourself, you are more likely to explore new opportunities, take on challenges that push you out of your comfort zone, and strive for excellence in everything you do. In contrast, when you lack self-belief, you may hesitate to try new things, second-guess your abilities, and settle for mediocrity.

Another benefit of self-belief is that it helps you build resilience. Life is full of ups and downs, and setbacks are inevitable. However, when you have self-belief, you are better equipped to handle and bounce back from these setbacks. You are less likely to let failure define or discourage you from pursuing your goals. Instead, you see setbacks as opportunities to learn, grow, and improve yourself.

Having self-belief also enables you to develop a more positive outlook on life. When you believe in yourself, you are more likely to see the good in every situation and have greater optimism about the future. This, in turn, makes you more resilient and better able to handle life's challenges. Furthermore, when you have a positive outlook on life, you are more likely to attract positive people and opportunities into your life.

In conclusion, self-belief is a crucial ingredient for success in life. It enables you to tap into your full potential, build resilience, develop a positive outlook on life, and achieve your goals. Therefore, it is essential to cultivate self-belief by acknowledging your strengths, learning from your failures, setting realistic goals, and surrounding yourself with positive influences. With self-belief, you can overcome any obstacle and achieve anything that you set your mind to.

Self-doubt through Midlife

Self-doubt is a common experience that can impact our lives in many ways. It can hold us back from pursuing our dreams, trying new things, or believing in ourselves. At its core, self-doubt is the negative voice in our heads that tells us we are not good enough, will fail, or should not even bother trying. These thoughts can be overwhelming and can prevent us from reaching our full potential.

To overcome self-doubt, we need to recognize and challenge those negative thoughts. This can be a complex process, but it is essential to build our self-belief. One way to do this is to practice positive self-talk. We can actively replace negative thoughts with positive ones when we notice negative thoughts creeping in.

For example, if we think, "I'm not good enough," we can counter that thought with, "I am talented and capable." We can shift our mindset and build our confidence by consciously focusing on positive reviews.

Another way to overcome self-doubt is to remind ourselves of our strengths and accomplishments. We can accomplish great things when we focus on what we have achieved. It can be helpful to list our achievements, no matter how small they seem. This can serve as a reminder that we have succeeded in the past and that we can do so again in the future.

It is also essential to focus on the possibilities rather than the limitations. When we are self-doubt, we may quickly concentrate on why we cannot do something. However, if we shift our focus to what is possible, we can open ourselves up to new opportunities and experiences. This requires a willingness to take risks and step outside our comfort zones, but the rewards can be significant.

Ultimately, building self-belief is a process that requires time and effort. It does not happen overnight, but with practice and persistence, we can overcome self-doubt and achieve our goals. We can approach challenges with confidence and resilience when we believe in ourselves. We can take on new opportunities and experiences with excitement and possibility. And most importantly, we can live our lives to the fullest, knowing that we have the power to achieve great things.

Embracing Failure at Midlife: Learning and Growing from Setbacks

In midlife, many of us face the reality that life doesn't always go according to plan. We may have experienced setbacks in our personal or professional lives that have left us feeling discouraged and defeated. Getting stuck in a cycle of negative thinking and self-doubt can be easy when things don't go as expected. However, embracing failure can help us break free from this mindset and learn to view setbacks as opportunities for growth and learning.

Failure is a natural part of life, and it is something that we all experience at some point. Whether it's a failed relationship, a business venture that didn't pan out, or a missed opportunity, we all have experienced setbacks that can be difficult to overcome. However, when we embrace failure, we can learn from our mistakes and use that knowledge to improve. We become more resilient and better equipped to handle challenges in the future.

To embrace failure, we must let go of the fear of failure and focus on the lessons learned. It's important to understand that failure does not reflect our worth as individuals. Instead, it's a part of the learning process and an opportunity to grow and develop. When we approach failure with a growth mindset, we can view it as a chance to learn and improve rather than a personal defeat.

One way to embrace failure is to reframe our mindset around it. Instead of viewing failure as a negative outcome, we can see it as a stepping stone to success. When we shift our focus from the result to the process, we can learn to appreciate the journey and the lessons learned along the way.

Another way to embrace failure is to practice self-compassion. It's natural to feel disappointed or frustrated when things don't go as planned. However, it's important to remember that we are all human and make mistakes. By practising self-compassion, we can learn to be kinder and more understanding towards ourselves and our failures.

In addition to reframing our mindset and practising self-compassion, seeking support from others is essential. Talking to friends or family about our failures can help us process our emotions and gain a fresh perspective. Additionally, seeking a mentor or coach can provide valuable guidance and support as we navigate difficult times.

In conclusion, embracing failure in midlife can be a powerful tool for learning and growth. By reframing our mindset, practising self-compassion, and seeking support from others, we can learn to view setbacks as opportunities for growth and development. When we embrace failure, we become more resilient and better equipped to handle challenges in the future. Remember, failure is not a defeat – it's a chance to learn and improve.

Avoid Procrastination

Procrastination is a typical behaviour observed in people of all ages. However, it can become particularly problematic during midlife. This is when individuals are often faced with numerous responsibilities, such as caring for ageing parents, managing their health concerns, and navigating changes in their personal and professional lives. With so much to do and so little time, procrastination can be tempting.

Procrastination can be particularly problematic during midlife because it can lead to increased stress and anxiety. When we put off important tasks, we may find ourselves scrambling to complete them at the last minute, feeling overwhelmed and frazzled. This can be especially true for midlife individuals who are already dealing with a lot of stressors. In addition, procrastination can lead to missed opportunities and unfulfilled goals, leaving us feeling regretful and dissatisfied with our lives.

Another reason why procrastination can be a problem during midlife is that it can lead to a sense of stagnation. When we put off important tasks, we may feel stuck in a rut, unable to move forward and make progress in our lives. This can be particularly frustrating for midlife individuals who may be experiencing a sense of dissatisfaction with their current circumstances. Procrastination can exacerbate these feelings, making finding motivation and taking action even more challenging.

Despite these challenges, there are strategies that midlife individuals can use to overcome procrastination. One approach is to break tasks down into smaller, more manageable steps. This can make daunting tasks feel less overwhelming and more achievable. Another strategy is to set specific goals and deadlines for completing tasks. This can create a sense of urgency and motivate us to take action. Finally, it can be helpful to identify the underlying causes of procrastination, such as fear of failure or a lack of confidence, and work on addressing these issues directly.

In conclusion, procrastination can be a common problem during midlife, but it is not impossible. By taking proactive steps to overcome this behaviour, midlife individuals can reduce stress, increase productivity, and find greater satisfaction in their personal and professional lives.

Discovering Your Purpose: Aligning Values, Passions, and Career Choices

In life's journey, we often find ourselves at a crossroads during middle age. The familiar path we have been treading seems uncertain, and questions about our purpose and fulfilment arise. This subchapter aims to guide men and women over 40 who are experiencing a midlife crisis, contemplating a career change, or seeking financial freedom, retirement concerns, or personal growth.

One of the critical aspects of navigating this midlife maze is aligning our values, passions, and career choices. It is essential to introspect and identify what drives us, what deals we hold dear, and what gives us a sense of fulfilment. Understanding our intrinsic motivations allows us to embark on a journey that aligns with our authentic selves.

Self-discovery becomes even more crucial for those in the public sector, retail, tourism, or health industries. These sectors often require individuals to serve others, and finding personal fulfilment within these roles can lead to a more meaningful career. However, assessing whether these roles align with our values, passions, and long-term goals is essential, especially if we find ourselves questioning our purpose.

Financial stability is another concern that often arises during midlife. As we contemplate a career change or explore new avenues, it is natural to wonder about the financial implications. This subchapter acknowledges the importance of economic freedom. It offers valuable insights on how to navigate this aspect of midlife crisis. It provides guidance on planning for retirement, managing finances during a career transition, and exploring opportunities that can lead to financial stability in the long run.

Furthermore, this subchapter recognises the significance of health and wellness during this transformative phase. Midlife crisis often prompts individuals to reevaluate their lifestyles, including physical and mental well-being. It explores the connection between self-discovery and health, emphasising the importance of self-care and personal growth to navigate the midlife maze successfully. It also delves into various wellness practices, such as yoga, meditation, and adopting new skills that can contribute to overall well-being.

In conclusion, "Discovering Your Purpose: Aligning Values, Passions, and Career Choices" is a subchapter that aims to guide men and women in their 40s and beyond through self-discovery during a midlife crisis. It addresses career change, financial stability, retirement, and health concerns, offering valuable insights and practical advice for navigating this transformative phase. We can find fulfilment and create a more purposeful life by aligning our values, passions, and career choices.

Cultivating Happiness: Finding Joy and Contentment in the Midlife Journey

In the hustle and bustle of our daily lives, it's easy to lose sight of what truly brings us happiness and contentment. As we navigate the journey of midlife, with its unique challenges and opportunities, it becomes increasingly important to cultivate a sense of joy and fulfilment. This subchapter explores strategies and insights to help men and women over 40 find happiness and contentment in their midlife journey.

One of the critical aspects of cultivating happiness in midlife is embracing the process of self-discovery. Many individuals experience a midlife crisis, a period of introspection and questioning, as they reassess their goals, values, and priorities. This subchapter delves into the transformative power of self-discovery, encouraging readers to explore their passions, interests, and values to unlock a more profound sense of fulfilment.

Financial concerns often loom large during midlife, particularly those contemplating a career change or retirement. This subchapter offers practical advice on achieving financial freedom, including budgeting, saving, and investing strategies. It also explores alternative career options and provides insights for those transitioning from the public sector, retail, tourism, or other industries, helping readers confidently navigate the financial landscape.

Health and wellness are crucial components of a happy and fulfilling midlife journey. This subchapter delves into the importance of self-care, stress management, and maintaining a healthy lifestyle. It explores the benefits of incorporating new skills and hobbies, such as yoga, to enhance overall well-being and promote a positive mindset.

Whether you're experiencing a midlife crisis, contemplating a career change, or simply seeking greater happiness and fulfilment in midlife, this subchapter offers valuable insights and guidance. By embracing self-discovery, achieving financial freedom, prioritizing health and wellness, and learning from the experiences of others, men and women over 40 can cultivate a deep sense of happiness and contentment as they navigate the journey of midlife.

Creating a Meaningful Life: Balancing Career, Relationships, and Personal Growth

In our fast-paced and ever-changing world, finding balance and meaning in our lives can seem like an elusive goal. As we navigate the challenges of midlife, it becomes even more crucial to strike a harmonious equilibrium between our careers, relationships, and personal growth. This subchapter will explore practical strategies and insights to help you create a meaningful life that encompasses these essential aspects.

Career Change: The midlife years often bring a desire for change and self-discovery. Whether unsatisfied with your current job or seeking new challenges, this is the perfect time to explore alternative career paths. We will delve into the career change process, guiding you in identifying your passions, acquiring new skills, and leveraging your existing experience to transition successfully. Additionally, we will address the concerns of public sector workers, retail professionals, tourism industry professionals, and others, offering specific advice tailored to these niches.

Financial Freedom: Financial stability is crucial to a meaningful life, especially as retirement concerns loom. We will discuss practical strategies for achieving financial freedom in midlife, including budgeting, investing, and planning for retirement. Whether facing economic instability due to a midlife crisis or simply seeking ways to maximize your resources, this subchapter will provide actionable tips to secure your financial future.

Relationships: Nurturing meaningful relationships is vital for overall well-being during midlife. We will delve into the complexities of maintaining healthy relationships, including romantic partnerships, friendships, and family dynamics. From communication skills to managing conflicts, we will explore strategies to foster strong connections and navigate the challenges that arise during this stage of life.

Personal Growth: Midlife is an ideal time for personal growth and self-discovery. We will explore various avenues for personal development, including health and wellness practices such as yoga. Discovering new hobbies, exploring creative outlets, and setting personal goals are essential to cultivating a fulfilling life. We will guide you on embracing unique growth opportunities and tapping into your inner potential.

Balancing your career, relationships, and personal growth can create a meaningful life that brings fulfilment and happiness. This subchapter will equip men and women over 40 to navigate a midlife crisis, seeking self-discovery, financial stability, and improved health and wellness, with the tools and insights needed to embark on this transformative journey. Through practical strategies and inspiring stories, "Midlife A True Journey" will empower you to embrace this stage of life and create a life that truly matters.

Chapter 9: Midlife Questions?

Top 30 Questions to reflect back on your life so far.

1. What have I accomplished so far?
2. What are my biggest regrets?
3. What are my greatest strengths?
4. What are my biggest weaknesses?
5. How have my relationships with others impacted my life?
6. Have I pursued my passions and interests?
7. What are my financial goals and how am I working towards them?
8. Have I taken care of my physical health?
9. What are my spiritual beliefs and how do they guide me?
10. What are my personal values and how do they shape my decisions?
11. Have I taken risks in my life?
12. How have I handled failure and setbacks?
13. What are my career goals and am I satisfied with my current job?
14. Have I made a positive impact on the world around me?

15. What are my goals for the future?
16. How do I define happiness?
17. What are my priorities in life?
18. What have I learned from my past experiences?
19. How have I grown and changed over time?
20. What are my hobbies and interests?
21. Have I travelled and explored new places?
22. What have I done to give back to my community?
23. How have I handled stress and adversity?
24. What are my biggest fears and how have I overcome them?
25. How have I supported my loved ones?
26. What have I done to continue learning and growing?
27. Have I taken time to reflect on my life and make changes when necessary?
28. What are my goals for my personal relationships?
29. Have I made peace with my past?
30. What legacy do I want to leave behind?

Take your time going through each question, try to give them as much thought as possible and write down your answers.

Congratulations on taking the time to reflect on your life by answering these thought-provoking questions. Through this process, you have better understood yourself and your life experiences. Perhaps you have discovered your greatest strengths and weaknesses or identified areas in your life that you wish to improve upon. You may have also gained clarity on your goals and priorities, both in your personal and professional life.

While reflecting on your regrets and fears may have been difficult, it is essential to remember that these experiences have helped shape who you are today. Acknowledging them has taken a crucial step towards personal growth and healing.

Your relationships with others have undoubtedly impacted your life, and it is vital to continue to nurture and strengthen these connections. Pursuing your passions and interests, caring for your physical health, and exploring new places are all important aspects of a fulfilling life.

As you move forward, reflecting on your values and how they inform your decisions is essential. By setting goals and taking risks, you can continue to grow and learn from your experiences. Remember to be kind to yourself as you navigate setbacks and failure and to take time to reflect and make changes as needed.

Ultimately, the legacy you leave behind is up to you. By living a life that aligns with your values and priorities and positively impacting those around you, you can create a meaningful and fulfilling life.

What now, What's on your bucket list?

As we reach middle age, we often reflect on our lives and the things we have yet to do. A bucket list of things that we want to experience before we "kick the bucket." For those approaching retirement or already retired, a bucket list can serve as a roadmap for the next chapter in life. Here are some ideas for unfulfilled dreams to add to your list:

1. **Travel to a new destination:** Whether it's a city you've always wanted to explore, a country you've never been to, or a natural wonder you've always wanted to see, travelling can be a great way to broaden your horizons and create new memories. Consider taking a road trip, booking a cruise, or even backpacking through a foreign land.
2. **Learn a new skill:** Retirement provides the perfect opportunity to pursue a hobby or learn a new skill you've always been interested in. This could be anything from playing an instrument, painting, or even learning a new language.
3. **Volunteer for a cause you care about:** Giving back to your community can be incredibly rewarding and fulfilling. Consider volunteering for a cause you are passionate about, such as animal rescue, environmental conservation, or working with underprivileged youth.
4. **Write a memoir or family history:** Sharing your life story or your ancestors' stories can be a great way to preserve your legacy and pass down important family history to future generations. Consider writing a memoir or interviewing family members to create a family history book.
5. **Start a business or pursue entrepreneurship:** Retirement can provide the flexibility and freedom to pursue your entrepreneurial dreams. Whether starting a new business, consulting, or freelancing, this can be a great way to stay engaged, keep your mind sharp, and generate income.

6. **Learn to cook a new cuisine:** Cooking can be a fun and creative outlet, and learning to cook a fresh cuisine can be a great way to expand your palate and impress your friends and family. Consider taking a cooking class or travelling to a new destination to learn about the local cuisine.

7. **Take up a new form of exercise:** Staying active and healthy is important at any age, but there is always time to try a new record. Consider taking up yoga, Pilates, or even martial arts.

8. **Learn to play a new sport:** Similarly, learning a new sport can be a great way to stay active and challenge yourself physically. Consider taking up golf, tennis, or even trying out a new water sport like paddleboarding or kayaking.

9. **Attend a significant event or festival:** From music festivals to sporting events, attending an important event or festival can be a fun and memorable experience. Consider attending events like the Olympics, Coachella, or a major sporting event like the Super Bowl or World Cup.

10. **Spend quality time with loved ones:** Finally, retirement provides the perfect opportunity to spend quality time with those you love. Consider taking a family vacation, hosting a reunion, or spending more time with your children and grandchildren.

Self-Care Practices: Self-care is not a luxury but a necessity, especially during midlife. It involves deliberately nurturing our mental, emotional, and physical well-being. This subchapter will explore self-care practices that can help individuals navigate the challenges of midlife with grace and resilience. We will delve into the importance of stress management, mindfulness, and relaxation techniques and introduce practices such as journaling, meditation, and engaging in hobbies that promote overall well-being.

Conclusion: By embracing healthy habits, such as proper nutrition, regular exercise, and self-care practices, men and women over 40 can enhance their overall health and reduce the risk of ageing illnesses. Whether navigating a midlife career change, seeking financial freedom, or concerned about retirement, prioritising your well-being is paramount. This subchapter will equip you with the knowledge and practical strategies to embrace a healthier lifestyle and navigate the midlife maze with confidence and vitality. Remember, there is always time to invest in yourself and prioritise your health and wellness.

In conclusion, a bucket list can be a great way to create a roadmap for the next chapter in life. Whether travelling to a new destination, learning a new skill, or spending quality time with loved ones, there are endless possibilities for unfulfilled dreams to add to your list. So get started today, and enjoy all that life has to offer!

Have Your Own **Midlife True Journey** and remember **Bestlife Is Midlife.**

BESTLIFEISMIDLIFE

Dear reader,

I am honoured to dedicate this book to the two most influential people: my beloved wife, Mandy, and my dear son, Josh. This book would never have come to fruition without their unwavering love, support, and encouragement.

The journey we have been on together has been filled with both joy and challenges, but through it all, we have remained steadfast in our commitment to one another. Mandy has been my rock, confidante, and partner in every sense of the word. Her unwavering love and support have sustained me through the toughest of times. I am forever grateful for her presence in my life.

Josh, my dear son, has been the light of my life since he was born. Watching him grow into the amazing person he is today has been one of the greatest joys of my life. His kindness, intelligence, and sense of humour always amaze me. I am proud he started his journey with multiple businesses at 18.

To both Mandy and Josh, I thank you from the bottom of my heart. Without your love, guidance, and unwavering support, I would not be who I am today. This book is a testament to the incredible journey we have all been on together, and I dedicate it to you with all my love.

Acknowledgements Page: *I want to take a moment to express my gratitude to the people and organizations that have been instrumental in the creation and publication of this book.*

Firstly, thank KDP for publishing my first book, "Midlife Wakeup Call," and now this latest book. Your support has been invaluable, and I am grateful for the opportunity to share my work with a broader audience.

I would also like to thank James Russell, whose Facebook advert inspired me to join Launch You. The program opened my eyes to the digital business world. It taught me valuable skills that have helped me in my journey.

I want to acknowledge my team of managers who, back in 2021, made me realise that I was putting work first and doing too many hours. I remember vividly sitting on a Cornish beach, and their words struck a chord. Thank you for looking out for me especially Simon Day and reminding me of the importance of work life balance.

Finally, I want to thank my wife, Mandy, for her unwavering support and encouragement. You have been by my side every step of the way, even when I was burning the midnight oil. Thank you for your love, patience, and understanding. To all those who have contributed to this book in one way or another, I am deeply grateful. Your support and encouragement have been invaluable, and I could not have done this without you.

Printed in Great Britain
by Amazon